THE HUSHED UP WORDS: THE WEIRD SEX CULTS AND RITUALS OF OUR WORLD

DR. RAINA S. PATTERSON

To all my readers

Contents

Foreword   *vii*

Preface   *ix*

Acknowledgements   *xi*

Prologue   *xiii*

1. Chapter 1   1

2. Chapter 2   4

3. Chapter 3   7

4. Chapter 4   10

5. Women's Breast Size Increases After Marriage, Is 14
   It?

6. Chapter 6   17

7. Chapter 7   22

8. Chapter 8   26

Foreword

Sex is a primitive human instinct. Whether it is your bedroom or any intimate moment, you too may go crazy with your partner for various crazy movements. But in the case of sex, this craziness is probably your own. There is no bizarre custom or custom behind it. But did you know that there are various customs regarding sex among different tribal groups of the world? And all these customs are absolutely bizarre. One will be amazed to proceed into this strange world of sex.

Preface

Tribal world

Sex is both a normal thing and also a taboo word. This book brings forth the hushed up words of sex into details. Not only tribal worlds but also civilised worlds have mant such things. This book opens up those hushed words.

Acknowledgements

All my teachers.

Prologue

The story of some strange sexual intercourse When having intercourse in the dark of night in the bedroom or by turning on the light, people do various experiments with their partner. Occasionally there is a change in the method of intercourse for a change of taste. There is a change in the posture of intercourse. In order to make the intercourse more exciting, there is a constant experimentation about the position of the person at the moment of intercourse. But there are some strange sex practices in the world that you may be surprised to know. In some remote areas of Austria, young women perform a traditional dance. On this occasion, the dancing women keep a piece of apple under their armpits and dance. At the end of the ceremony, the women go to the man of their choice and pass the apple to him. If the man eats the piece of apple, it means that the man is willing to have sex with the woman. After that, the couple started having reckless sex. And if the man returns the apple, then there is no possibility of sexual intercourse between them. The woman approached the other man with a piece of apple. In the Mahabharata, Draupadi was the only wife of the five brothers of the Pandavas. Patterns of this same phenomenon are found in some tribes of Nepal. In this tribe of Nepal, it is customary for all the sons of the house to marry one woman. The reason is, of course, very strange. That is why all the brothers get married to one woman so that there is no more share in the property. And so the men of this tribe do not believe in giving birth to more children. Mangaia Island at the southernmost tip of the Cook Islands. An autonomous island nation independent of New Zealand in the South Pacific. The island is famous for its strange sexual tradition. Older women have sex with younger men on Mangaiya Island. Young people are first asked to have sex with older women to teach them how to please their partner. In ancient Greece, married and unmarried adult men had intercourse with teenagers. However, intercourse with children was not allowed. Adult men used to have sex with teenagers, usually between the ages of 15 and 19. Cambodia's Kreung tribe builds a hut for the mating of teenage girls in their community. But the funny thing is, every day different boys come to this hut and spend one night. When the girl announces that she has found a suitable partner, then the anagona of different boys stops. Odabe tribesmen of Niger in West Africa are married off at an early age. After that, when they grow up, men wear makeup at the annual Gereol festival and wear other men's clothes.

Sex is a primitive human instinct. Whether it is your bedroom or any intimate moment, you too may go crazy with your partner for various crazy movements. But in the case of sex, this craziness is probably your own. There is no bizarre custom or custom behind it. But did you know that there are various customs regarding sex among different tribal groups of the world? And all these customs are absolutely bizarre. You will be amazed to hear that. Let's take a look at some of the practices. 1. Zambian Tribes: In the case of the Zambian tribes of New Guinea, boys and girls are separated when they are 6 years old. This separation lasts for 10 years. And in these 10 years, they have been piercing their noses and ears. No, it doesn't end there. There are more. The biggest surprise is that for the last 10 years they have had to drink the semen of the strongest fighters of the Zambian group. 2. Trobriander tribe: In this tribe of Papua New Guinea, boys and girls engage in sexual activity at a very young age. Boys engage in sexual activities between the ages of 10 and 12. The girls are even younger there. Girls of this tribe engage in sex work when they are only 6 years old. 3. Mangaiya Tribe: Mangaiya is an island in the South Pacific Ocean. The custom here is for young boys to have sex with older women. Only 13-year-old boys have sex with women much older than them. 4. Austria: There is a strange custom about sex in a remote area of Austria. Here women dance with apple slices under their armpits. And after the dance, they let their male partner eat that piece of apple. 5. Kreang Tribe: The people of this tribe build a house in Cambodia. Whose name is 'Love Hat'. The teenage girls of the tribe come to this 'Love Hut' and have sex with different men until they find a partner of their choice. 6. In ancient Greek civilization, there was no such thing as being attracted to the opposite sex for sex. In that case one man would have sex with another man. 6. There are several tribes in Nepal where all the boys in a house, the Thudi brothers, marry only one girl. And all the brothers have sex with that one woman. 8. Odabe Tribe: Odabe is a tribe in the Niger region of West Africa. This is a festival held every year in Niger. And in that festival, the men of the tribe wear stolen makeup and colorful clothes. But it is very strange how he wears clothes. Gora fled with another's wife in Bengal. 9. You have heard of many strange events in ancient Egypt. Here are some weird things about Egyptian sex. The ancient Egyptians thought that masturbation was the only reason the water of the Nile flowed well. And that is why the ancient Egyptians used to give their semen in the Nile river in the open field. And it was celebrated as a festival. 10. In Indonesia, it is customary to have sex with any person other than one's own partner during the Pon celebration. It is said that having sex with someone other than one's own partner at the festival seven times a year fulfills all their desires. 11. Both men and women wear their underwear while having sex on the island of Inisbeg, Ireland.

CHAPTER ONE

24 strange sexual desires of women! Physical intimacy or sexuality is the inevitable consequence of almost all love. In general, women are upset about this, but still they do not say anything openly. However, in many cases, women are not lagging behind men in the case of strange 'asexual fantasies', even if they cannot say anything openly. Rather, they are ahead. A British website conducted a survey of women around the world on how to get involved in bodybuilding. The women were asked about their most bizarre sexual fantasies. In that survey, various strange desires have come up. From that, we have chosen the 24 strangest desires of women- 1. Some women like to be close to the cinema. If the men agree, they agree. 2. Many people want to kiss on the forehead or cheek after sexual intercourse. 3. If the male partner becomes reckless as soon as the bedroom door is closed, then many people also like

that. 4. Four reunion after reunion! Many also want it. They say that this Four Play-E may become the beginning of reunion once again. 5. There may be various tensions in life. However, no woman wants to talk about them during the meeting. . Many masked women also like violent intercourse like scratching. . Many people like to inform the neighbors indirectly that they are enjoying the reunion. This means that during the intimacy, he informs everyone with a reckless shout. . Some people want the whole reunion to be standing still. 10. Many people can't think of getting close without romantic songs. 11. The caress starts in the drawing room, from there in the bedroom, and finally in the bathroom - many women also like that sex. 12. Some very romantic women love to have sex between essential oils and flower petals in the bathtub. 13. Some people imagine that their partner will throw her in the air during sex. Take care again. 14. Thus fashionable. But no woman wants to think about whether the bed is clean or tidy during sex. 15. Sex time: Not the phone. In most cases, women are reluctant to pick up the phone. 16. During sex, some people love to shout the name of the partner again. 16. Many people enjoy sex by keeping an eye on it. 16. As long as sex, kiss. Many people want this kind of romantic reunion. 19. Some women prefer sex in a moving car. 20 Many people want their male partner to be awkward to undress during sex. 21. Many women enjoy sex by interrupting their partner's emergency work. 22. Almost everyone enjoys long term reunion. 23. There are also women who want to be reunited with melted candles. 24. Many women love to meet under the influcnce of alcohol.

CHAPTER TWO

Do you know about the five weirdest sex problems
Ordinary people are just as excited about sex as those who
have some strange sexual problems. Healthy normal sex

life is desirable for everyone. Sex is also a very important part of love or marriage. But those who have some strange sexual problems, they are always terrified about it. Even though they realize that sex is not very pleasant for them, it becomes very difficult to explain it to their partner. Some people have strange problems about which others have no idea. Find out about some of these problems. Endless orgasm Who doesn't like orgasm? If both parties have an orgasm during sexual intercourse, there is nothing more pleasurable than that. So when you hear someone having an endless orgasm, it will feel as if he has got the moon in his hand. But the disease is not so pleasant at all. On the contrary. Many girls have this problem. This disease is called persistent genital arousal disorder. It has nothing to do with sexual desire. Such an organ is out of their control. Such a situation can happen suddenly. And one orgasm after another. If it sounds good, it can be quite painful physically. There is also a risk of stagnation of limbs. Sexomania Many people walk in their sleep. If the problem is serious, he does various things while sleeping. But those who are able to have sex in their sleep, their problem is called sexomnia. The disease is quite confusing. Such people can read legal issues especially about sexual harassment. The words about sex are never said to girls Retrograde ejaculation Men have orgasms, but the sperm did not come out? Is that even possible? Although the body is producing enough sperm, it is moving to the bladder during orgasm. This disease is called retrograde ejaculation. According to doctors, this disease is not supposed to be a physical complication. But for couples trying to conceive, the disease can be a curse. Phimosis Many people feel suffocated when wearing a turtleneck sweater. This disease is a lot like that. But the pain is much more. The skin on the outside of the genitals of men is so hard that it looks like a rubber band has been put on the head of the genitals. This situation is quite difficult. Sexual intercourse can also be fatal. Therefore, doctors advise to remove it through surgery. Physical illness after orgasm After orgasm, sleep in peace with your partner? This is an ideal situation for many. But those who have this rare disease, their condition is very different. This disease is called post orgasmic illness syndrome. Flu-like symptoms appear immediately after ejaculation. Fever may come. No cure for this disease has yet been found. However, in order to bring the situation under control, there is a trend of thinning one's own sperm and giving it to the body through injection.

CHAPTER THREE

The words about sex are never said to girls Many kinds of expectations are created in the minds of girls about sex. But if you know a few things bcforc that, many confusions can be removed. Movies, story books, magazines, friends chat, various discussions about sex from adolescence. Listening to them, various expectations are created in the minds of girls about sex without knowing it. However, there is no discussion on the issues that can be beneficial if they are known in advance. Not at school-college, or at home. Sex is still a taboo subject in our society. Lack of open discussion also creates various confusions. So it is necessary to know some things in advance. That person is not the most important person in the first sex Like first love, for the first time sex is more romanticized in the society. The first time girls learn to think, it will be a great experience. Whoever will be with him will also become one of the most important person in life. In fact, it may not be. Maybe at an early age you started having sex with someone who changed a lot later. The relationship broke down and he went on his way. That person is nowhere in your life. That is the most normal. Your sexual needs will change with age The kind of outfit you liked at the age of 20, after 30 years, maybe the outfit is not being liked at all. So is sexual desire. As you grow older, your desires will change. There is no need to worry about this. Sexual intercourse is not the end of the relationship Feeling we have 'Run out of gas' emotionally. But does that mean you are very close? There are many sides to intimacy. Just being physically close means that the two have very similar minds — it may not be. Don't be surprised by this. Your sexual needs may be higher Is your sexual desire higher than your partner's? Maybe. Don't just blame yourself for it. Or don't think you have a problem. Not all people have the same hunger and sleep, nor can their sexual needs be the same. Many people are exaggerating about sex life Got upset about having sex with school-college friends? It seems that everyone's life is full except you? Do not grieve for lies. Be aware that teens tend to exaggerate their sex lives. Most people are inexperienced at this time. So they have not yet had the time to set a standard for what is a pleasant experience or what is not. So don't take anything for granted.

CHAPTER FOUR

Boy's genitals are being worshiped, find out about the weird genre of 'Penis Festival' Every day more than one festival is being celebrated in one of the cities of the world. Throughout the year, people from different communities come together for various festivals. This time the Japanese got involved in a strange festival. In Japan, the Penis Festival is celebrated mainly by married couples and sex workers. Crowds of hundreds of people across the city. The image is much the same as when everyone carries the idol of the goddess on their shoulders during the puja. Some people are carrying idols on their shoulders. Everyone's behavior is saying that a festival is being celebrated. Going closer, seeing the statue, the eye-catching tree. It is a statue in the shape of a man's genitals. Surprising but true. The 'Penis Festival' is being celebrated in Japan today. It is called 'Kanamara Matsuri' in Japanese. In a word, it is a gender festival. This festival is celebrated on the first Sunday of April every year. In Japan, there are more people from the Shinto community. They celebrate the festival centered on Kanayama Hiko and Kanayama Him. This 'Penis Festival' is a prayer for sexual health. Every day more than one festival is being celebrated in one of the cities of the world. Throughout the year, people from different communities come together for various festivals. This time the Japanese got involved in a strange festival. In Japan, the Penis Festival is celebrated mainly by married couples and sex workers. Unmarried men also joined the festival. This festival is celebrated in Kanayama temple. Inside the exhibition hall of the temple, pictures, symbolic objects and books of sexual tradition are kept. The program begins with a parade. A fun parade called 'Kanamara Boat Mikoshi' was first held. Then there is a ritual called 'Mochi Nage'. At the end of the puja, Shinto priests stood on a high platform and threw rice cakes into the crowd. Supposedly, this cake is a symbol of fertility. So if you can catch it, you will get

God's blessing. The temple's proceeds from the festival are donated to research on HIV. It is known that newlyweds come to this temple if they have sexual problems. It is said that Rakshaan was hiding in the vagina of a woman. So anyone who had sex with her would die. Then a man made an iron penis and had intercourse with that woman. Then the monster's teeth are cut. An iron penis is placed in front of the Kanayama temple to commemorate this story. So by going around this temple and celebrating the festival of 'Kanamara Matsuri', everyone's sexual problems are removed.

Women's breast size increases after marriage, is it?

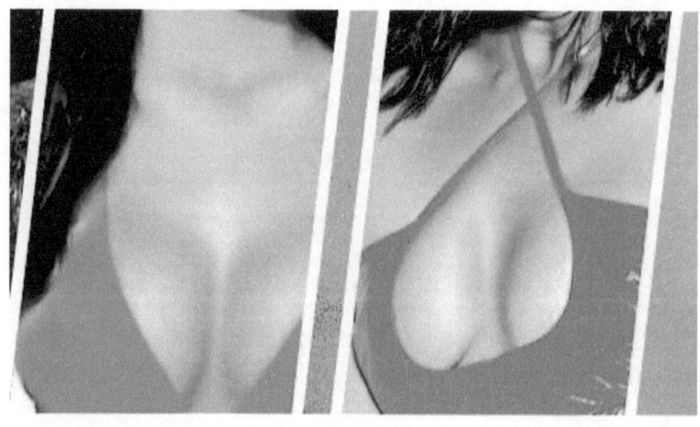

Women's breast size increases after marriage, is it at all? Know the truth A few days before the wedding, the girl starts using expensive creams and cosmetic products to make herself look beautiful, because every girl dreams of looking different and the most beautiful in her wedding. Every boy and girl in the world knows that one day they will get married. Marriage is considered the most sacred relationship. Boys and girls face many questions about the relationship between their future spouses and their nature. Most of the girls are excited about this marriage. A few days before the wedding, the girl starts using expensive creams and cosmetic products to make herself look beautiful, because every girl dreams of looking different and the most beautiful in her wedding and everyone wants to look her best. So that everyone sees him and appreciates him. What causes breast enlargement? Many believe that the reason for the increase in the size of the breasts of girls after marriage is the close relationship with their husbands. However, science has not yet confirmed this fact. A special survey was conducted. After marriage, women are surveyed about why their breasts get bigger and what their lifestyle is like. In this study, scientists conducted a study on married and unmarried girls. It has been observed that unmarried girls take great care of their health and fitness before marriage. Then after marriage the responsibility on them increases so much that they do not have time to take care of their health. Then they gradually gain weight. In addition, after the wedding, the in-laws often invite the newlyweds for dinner, which spoils their eating habits and makes them gain more weight than before. It happens when many girls start dieting and exercising before marriage. So that their figure looks best on the wedding day and the clothes they wear are different. Have you ever noticed that even thin girls get fat after marriage? The reason for this must have been understood this time. You too must be looking for the answer to the question, what could be the cause of sudden weight gain in girls. Not only that, after marriage, the girl's appearance and waist changes a lot. Just remember that a girl's size increases only when she is with her partner. The more time you spend with your partner.

CHAPTER SIX

Strange sexual laws in some countries of the world Sex is one of the most sensitive issues. Although in some countries this biological need has been taken in a simple way and in some countries it has been taken just the opposite. Strict laws have been enacted in several countries to prevent sex abuse. Moreover, from the religious point of view, separate restrictions have been issued to control this biological need. Even then, the lawmakers of some countries, the religious scholars of foreign countries, the thinkers have enacted all these bizarre laws and regulations in the name of controlling sex, which is ridiculous. Today, I am sharing with the respected bloggers about the anti-creation and inconsistent sex laws created by the legislators and religious scholars of some of these countries in the world. 1. Guam is an island in the Pacific Ocean, not the United States. The island of Guam is legally prohibited from marrying virgins. If a virgin girl wants to get married there, according to the law, she has to go to a man to give up her virginity. There are professional men here who are paid to destroy the virginity of virgin girls. 2. Washington law in the United States prohibits sexual intercourse with virgin girls. Husband will not be able to have intercourse with his virgin bride even on the night after marriage. However, no legal explanation has been given as to how a virgin girl can renounce her virginity, as has been the case with the virgin girls of Guam. 3. There are no legal restrictions on Lebanese men having sex with pets. However, the condition is that the animal that will have sex with the animal must be a female species, otherwise the maximum punishment for breaking the law may be death. 4. In some Middle Eastern countries, it is legal to have sex with sheep or goats. However, under no circumstances should a goat that has sexual intercourse be allowed to eat its meat. In this regard, the fatwa says, "After having sexual intercourse with a sheep, eating its meat is a grave sin." 5. Under Bahraini law, gynecologists can examine women's genitals. But in order to prevent accidents due to arousal, the legislators forbade the doctors to see the genitals directly and in that case they used mirrors to allow the patient to see and examine the genitals through reflection. . Islam forbids seeing the genitals of a dead person. The same conditions apply to those who take part in the bathing and burial of the dead. And for this reason, while bathing, bathing is done by placing a piece of brick or a piece of wood on the genitals of the corpse. 6. According to the law of the Cali region of Colombia, after the marriage of a girl child, she has to spend the night with her husband in the presence of her mother. . In Virginia, USA, having sex with an electric light is legal. 9. In the U.S. state of Utah, sexual intercourse with girls inside an ambulance is prohibited. If a girl is caught or proved to be doing this, then by law all the notoriety including the picture of that girl will be published in the local newspaper. On the other hand, in the case of men, it is revealed that "seven murders are forgiven". 10. There are no religious restrictions on sex in Hong Kong. However, if a wife thinks that her husband has cheated on her or if she finds evidence that her husband is an adulterer, then she can kill her husband only with her own hands. 11. Bolivia's Santa Cruz law makes it illegal for a man to have sex with a girl and her mother at the same time. 12. Arizona and Wisconsin in the United States have banned the wearing of clothing that reveals the erection of the penis. 13. Masturbation is a huge crime in Indonesia and the penalty for this crime is death. 14. In Minnesota, it is illegal for a man to have sex with a fish. 15. Oral sex is completely illegal in Singapore if it is not followed by vaginal intercourse.

CHAPTER SEVEN

We are not talking about Draupadi of Mahabharata in our own way. This is exactly what is happening in the twentieth century. Not only one girl, the whole village has five, six, seven husbands of one woman. Their context and history are completely different from that of Draupadi in the Mahabharata. This practice is practiced among the tribes in some parts of the Punjab province of India. The growing land crisis among the poor and the declining proportion of females compared to males is increasing day by day. And for all these reasons, in their married life, the Mahabharata has turned them into the characters of the five-Pandava story. In this village, seven or eight siblings are sharing a woman as their wife. In practice, such practices were common in ancient times among the Tians community of Kerala and the Tibetan tribes. The presence of these tribes in the foothills of the Himalayas in the twenty-first century in the Indian state of Punjab, such an event is not exactly digestible. However, the crisis of cultivable land, the scourge of poverty and the consequent decline in the proportion of female population have forced the population to adhere to this practice. In recent times, the ratio of females to males in Punjab has been calculated at 693 females per 1000 males. In this situation, half a dozen brothers of each family are marrying one woman at a time to prevent the decrease in the amount of land. The claims of government sources, however, are different. They say the situation is due to the alarming decline in the number of Sikh women marrying in the rural areas of present-day Punjab. The tradition has been going on for the last century that all the brothers in the family have to marry a woman. The land they have is divided among the boys. Later, when they get married, the land is passed on to the next generation. But since each brother has only one wife, the land is not likely to be divided separately in everyone's name. However, as a result, there has been an outbreak of unavoidable and inevitable child marriage among them and at the same time alarming rate of premature motherhood. But the power of women here is different. The names of Rajjo Verma's five husbands - Sant Ram, Bajju, Gopal, Guddu, Dinesh. Rajjo is happily married with five husbands and two children. The locals also said that there was no unrest among them. Similarly, another woman named Sunita Devi is happily married. She has two husbands. Her two husbands are also brothers. One is named Ranjit Singh, the other is named Chander Prakash. Rajjo has maintained the old tradition of the village. Who Rozzo will be with every night is entirely her decision. This is the custom there. Rajjo has two children. As a result of this custom, people here have no problem sharing property. In the words of Sunita, a resident of the village, she is very lucky. Because she is the wife of two husbands. One helps him cook and the other makes the baby man. Buddhi Devi also married two brothers in the same way. He is now about 60 years old. One of her husbands died. Another is still alive. However, in order to prevent this situation, many people in those areas nowadays get married in the neighboring states of Bihar and Uttar Pradesh, but the village religious leaders and socialists are obstructing them. They think that the children that will be born in their womb as a result of marrying girls from outside their society and culture will be inferior to the real Punjabis. Here the birth rate of daughters is comparatively much lower while in many cases it is seen that a married wife is being forced to have relations with other brothers of the husband against her will. The matter has also come under the scrutiny of the National Human Rights Commission of India and the National Commission for Women. They also feel that the women of these regions are not willingly accepting this mental and physical suffering at all, the strong social pressure and the insurmountable obligation of family poverty are forcing them to accept this practice without any hesitation. In contrast, the number of men who have crossed the age of marriage in government documents is increasing day by day. The situation in rural areas of Punjab including Bathinda, Mansa Muktsar, Sangrur, Faridkot and surrounding areas is alarming. However, even though that large number of men are unmarried in government and in a sense socially, they are not at all deprived of the taste of what is called straight Bengali or conjugal life. Each of these unmarried men is sharing the wife of one of the brothers in his family. There are two classes of farmers in the rural areas of Ludhiana and Jalandhar in Punjab. A class is the owner of huge real estate. They have huge farms or farms with air-conditioned state-of-the-art offices, imported BMWs, expensive cars including Lexus for transportation. In their lifestyle, the traditional traditions of Punjab are covered with thick western culture. In the interest of maintaining religious-social-cultural customs and clan or tribal nobility, they do not have to go through any complications in the necessary rituals and way of life. And the other class is like the mangatari farmers in our rural areas. Some of them have a small amount of land but most of them are landless agricultural laborers or day laborers. They have been compelled to practice the Pandava-Draupadi theory in order to prevent any small amount of real estate from being squandered. And for those who do not have even a little bit of land, the matter has become more compelling. There are many advantages as well as advantages to the villagers in this ongoing process.

CHAPTER EIGHT

What is the relationship between weight gain and sex, what experts say, Because it has been a common practice for a long time that girls get fat after marriage. The real reason behind this is still unclear. Many people say that if you have regular sex, you will gain weight. What is really so, what the experts say. Everyone has different fantasies about sex. Many people enjoy sex in different ways. But do you know that intercourse is not only a physical satisfaction, but also an infallible cure for the disease. It has been a common practice for a long time that girls get fat after marriage. The real reason behind this is still unclear. According to many, girls gain weight as a result of regular intercourse. Although according to science, it is not at all. Marriage has nothing to do with girls getting fat and having sex. And no one gets fat if they have regular sex. This idea is completely unscientific. According to experts, it is true that many people become obese after marriage. This is because of hormonal changes. After marriage, the body of girls becomes heavy. Especially the waist, thighs, chest, buttocks change shape. One of the reasons for this is the various changes in the sex hormones in the body. Many have the emotional satisfaction of being fat again. In addition to physical intercourse in a happy married life, weight gain is also possible in peace of mind. Many have the emotional satisfaction of being fat again. In addition to physical intercourse in a happy married life, weight gain is also possible in peace of mind. In order to keep the marriage strong, you have to be perfect not only physically, but also mentally and physically. Otherwise the danger will increase.